Acknowledgments

First and foremost, I humbly thank Jesus(God) for saving my life. I will never doubt nor deny you. Thank you for our peace of marriage.

Thank you, mom and dad, for bringing me to life. I will always love you both unconditionally. This book came to fruition because of my friendship with Belinda Olivas. Vanessa White inspired me to write. Accomplished writer, Ernesto Patino, gave me guidance and advice. Lamar Mathurin was nice enough to create the amazing art work. Don Miguel Ruiz' book, changed my way of thinking. My clients of twenty-three years, bring me purpose.

People need people. God created us all in his image.

Tales of the Marked Hand

David Galindo Rivera

STORIES SHOULD BE LIKE MOVIES... ARE YOU READY?

Forty-one years ago, a powerful curandero told my grandma, "I could never be harmed."

In the 1970's, the Mexican American community of El Paso, Texas was poor to middle class. The predominant religion was Catholic. Many also believed in curanderismo or faith healing. The ancient Toltecs had an ideology of peace and love. They were *supposedly* gifted with amazing abilities to heal. Their roots followed with generations of healing curanderos. She was powerful and revered in the community because she was psychic. My grandma believed in Jesus and in her. She told my mom. My mom eventually told me.

Curanderos have always been painted as *helpful healing* people. One such episode of *La Bamba* is when the curandero gave a necklace to Richie Valenzuela. He instructed Richie to *always* wear it to stay alive. Then, Richie's jealous brother tears it off during a fight. Shortly after, Richie dies in the infamous plane crash along with Buddy Holly and other musicians!

So, what was she thinking???

Growing up in El Paso was normal. Discipline was always stressed. No one is perfect, but my parents did their best. I will always honor and love them.

For college, I chose to live in Austin Texas. I am still here. Being a young adult had many trials and tribulations.

My 1st jobs were as a bouncer and uncertified trainer. They established the journey of my life to come. Being a bouncer reminded me of ego, but personal training set the path toward humility. In the early 90's, my brother and I worked at a night club, *Mirage*. I remember when the Egyptian club owner looked at us and said, "You both are hired!" I could not blame him. We were *imposing* young men. We soon gained respect. In El Paso, respect is valued. Fending for yourself is a rite of passage. My brother and I became legendary bouncers working at clubs in downtown Austin. Respect by force is the way of the conqueror. Jesus was *never* forceful.

Personal training at World gym allowed me to intimately connect with various personalities. I was helping people to spiritually and physically lift. Spiritually lifting brings light into darkness. One that is *continuously* surrounded by darkness will find it *more* difficult to see the light. Meanwhile, I craved being feared. This *dark* desire resulted in many fights including becoming a professional mixed martial artist. I had grandiose thoughts and beliefs. In 1999, I was featured in a documentary. It was about me trying to become a professional mixed martial arts fighter. I was humiliated because I lost. Believe it or not, this documentary made it to Netflix. So thousands of people have seen me get my ass kicked! I went into a deep depression because my ego was hurt. To cope, I resorted to drugs, alcohol and more fights. I was arrested for reckless driving and driving while intoxicated. Trying to redeem myself, I took fights against feared opponents. I was a fearless drug-taking demon.

Meanwhile, the gym continued to be a refuge. It was easy to introduce new members to nautilus machines and free weights. My confidence and friendliness impressed the gym owners. They soon promoted me to night manager. The gym energy at night was great. I started to meet unfriendly people though. I will never forget the *one* member. She was furious because I would not train her exclusively.

She angrily whispered something and shook her head toward me. A lot of religions are vengeance based. I pray for those who glorify violence. The next night, I fell through a glass case almost severing my femoral artery. They were replacing floor tiles in my receptionist area. I was spotting a member and ran back to a ringing phone. Trying to get back over the counter; I freakishly fell into a nearby glass case. The surgeon told me, I came 2 centimeters close to the artery. I was devastated but relieved to be alive. My leg recovered remarkably fast. Within three months, I was back to working in gyms. I have a passion for helping people get fit!

Next, Future Firm hired me as their night manager. I became professionally certified as a personal trainer; and started competing as an amateur bodybuilder. A wonderful woman named, Ninette Winston, hired me to work for her company, High Tech Bodies. God bless her.

One of my clients was a licensed massage therapist. After one of our sessions, she respectfully asked me to work on her shoulders. As soon as I put my hands on her, she said *"I had it."* Within a few minutes, her shoulder pain was gone. She recommended that I become a licensed massage therapist. After graduating from UT at Austin in 1998, I enrolled at Lauterstein-Conway massage school. Massage school felt like a union of healers working together to learn more. It was an amazing experience. Thank you, David Lauterstein and John

Conway. Human touch is so important. People need human contact and communication. I have an ability to *channel away* negative energy and pain. This became more powerful with experience.

Because of the terrorist attack of 09/11/2001, I was overcome with fear and hate. It was a dark time. I regretted not attending West Point. I investigated enlisting into the military. Previous injuries from fights disqualified me. This has been happening around the world for centuries. Invasions and war will create fear and hate for generations! I preferred to fear during this dark time.

LIVING IN FEAR IS LIVING IN THE PRESENT WITH SATAN!

In 23 years as a personal trainer, I have worked with many wonderful people. Belinda Olivas contacted me through Facebook because we went to the same high school. She wanted me to help her son. He was thinking of competing in a bodybuilding contest. She asked me how much I would charge her, and I said, "not to worry." I felt her distress and loneliness. I helped her son, but something told me to stay in touch with her. I would check on her and sometimes offer therapeutic massage. She would always respectfully decline. Then one day, she was hurting. I offered her bodywork and she finally accepted. I was surprised how beautiful and innocent she was. She was shy but strong in her convictions. So, we became friends. She would come once a month. I never charged her. She became comfortable enough to ask me personal questions. The first question was about my relationship with God. I remember how I felt. I was uncomfortable. I knew something existed but always kept my distance. My memories growing up with religion were not positive. I went to a Catholic school as a child and remember being spanked by the nun. Going to church was always a show. People would watch to see who came the best dressed. It was a popularity contest. I remember the money bowl always being passed around.

Religion has always been an institution. People need the community of church. It gives them a sense of belonging. This is good. Church leaders sometimes speak out against certain issues such as homosexuality and the other religions. It always bothered me, as well as, the business of religion. Jesus never classified people. He loved all people. He also despised people using his father's temple to make money! There is nothing wrong with two people loving each other regardless of gender or religion. Belinda has a passion for Jesus Christ. She would bring her bible and read scripture to me. I was always open to it. She would also go to the arch and minister to the homeless people. She fed them salty snacks, bananas and water. I previously judged them as mentally ill drug addicts. She is known as the *angel of the streets*. She always went by herself. For safety, I started to go along with her after the massage. She always felt pain free and energized afterwards. It was amazing to see her minister to the homeless. She reminded me of Jesus. I am thankful for all my clients. They learn from me and I learn from them. God bless them all.

GOD CREATED EVERYTHING THROUGH HIM, NOTHING WAS CREATED EXCEPT THROUGH HIM. (John 1:3)

April 5th, 2015 is the most important day of my life. Around 1:30pm, I drove to Saint Austin Catholic Church and prayed. I truthfully accepted Jesus as my lord and savior. As I drove away from the church, I will never forget the sudden rush of euphoric bliss and power. Something wonderful entered my soul because I have true faith. I asked God to heal my body. He said ok but, you will start working for me. Of course, I accepted. I was instructed to forgive those who had wronged me and then, to forgive myself. This is necessary to receive our Lord. *Holding grudges and guilt lessen the vibration of our spirit.* I decided to fill my mind with good works and holy scripture. I started with "The Four Agreements" by Don Miguel Ruiz. The four agreements are: Be impeccable with your word;[1] Don't take anything personally;[2] Don't make assumptions[3] and always do your best.[4] It's fascinating this was an ideology of an ancient civilization. The Toltecs are the descendants of current faith healers or curanderos. If all civilizations had adopted this ideology, our world would be completely different today. Where do you think this ideology came from?

---

[1] Don Miguel Ruiz, The Four Agreements(Amber-Allen Publishing; 1997); p.29
[2] P.53
[3] P.69
[4] P.83

I read the Holy Bible every other year. I am currently reading it for the third time. Reading the bible two times, has completely transformed my brain chemistry. I can't watch or hear anything that glorifies Satan. I shun it.

THE FEAR OF THE LORD IS WISDOM, AND TO SHUN EVIL IS UNDERSTANDING. (Job 28:28)

This was the beginning of my renewal; and the tipping point towards peace and love. It's important to share passions with others when it's intent is good. Who knows what would have happened to me without Belinda? I would be lost and still be addicted to opiates and alcohol. Accepting Jesus has truly saved my life...

Because of my film past, my clients wanted me to start a reality comedy gym series. I thought up the name *On Your Back*. They thought it was ingenious and funny. It was almost in the works, when I had an instance with Belinda during a session. We were almost toward the end of our session and she was face up. She said, "Do you know God is with us." I said, "Sure." She then said, "Look at up at the ceiling." I looked up and there I saw the outline of a cross. As I stared, I realized our bodies are temples of God's creation. We are him. Loving him is loving ourselves. We are all precious parts of our Lord. God is love. He is passion. He is everything good. We are all *one* with him once we accept him. I had already accepted Jesus but now I had a clear purpose. Belinda was *ON YOUR BACK* glorifying the cross that represents Christ and his suffering for all our sins! We are nothing without our Lord Almighty. We must always put him first and trust him. This is all we have. My mind, body and soul went through this amazing transformation after realizing this. It is still happening today.

The 1st episode of *On Your Back* premiered on August 18th, 2015. Instead of being a comedy, it was a short film about living God's dream! One part is about a client, Terry and his passion for finding natural plants to treat illness. These *God made* nutrients are purified plants made potent by distilling. Terry has used natural supplements and essential oils to keep himself healthy from a terminal illness. Sharing helpful passions with others is living God's dream! Belinda showcased her passion for Christ by helping the homeless after my massage.

The next year was dedicated to reading the bible again. The bible is always different with every reading. My brain chemistry has changed from reading scripture and positive works. I broke up with my girlfriend because she was unhappy. True love is merciful and unselfish. I love her. Today she is happy, and I am smiling for her!

In 2016, I experienced things most would not understand or believe. One night, I was drinking too much red wine. I boldly proclaimed my faith and love towards my Lord Almighty by asking to be challenged by Satan!

"ASK AND IT WILL BE GIVEN TO YOU; SEEK AND YOU WILL FIND; KNOCK AND THE DOOR WILL BE OPENED TO YOU."(Matthew 7:7)

It was a gloomy Saturday in mid-January. I was driving for Uber to keep myself busy. There was a rave near the airport. I will never forget the energy of the day. It was dark with a low vibration. I had already taken two passengers to the rave. I was surprised of all the millennials. They were barely dressed and high of ecstasy amongst other drugs. I am not judgmental but they all looked lifeless. I remember the days when I used to take MDMA and wanted to dance and love everyone around me. But, I did notice a lot of pretty girls. As I thought about the pretty girls, an instant Uber ride request manifested. The east Austin house had a lot of *lifeless looking young* people hanging around it. Suddenly out of nowhere, a friendly guy jumped into my car. I forgot his name, but he was headed back to that rave. We talked about the gloomy weather and all the young millennials at the rave. Then, we talked about all the beautiful uninhibited young girls. Suddenly, I see an iPhone appear to the right side of my face. I witnessed numerous photos of the same guy with orgies of beautiful women. He was laughing naming the women and describing how he had sex with each of them. I couldn't believe it and had a hard time focusing on my driving. I asked him how he did it because he was just average looking. He said, "Very easy David. All you have to do is JOIN

ME!" When I realized what he had asked me, I looked at my rear-view mirror. I saw what appeared to be a face with pointed up eyebrows and cat eyes.

"You could have beautiful women all day long!" "All you have to do is renounce God and sell your soul to me." "My name as you know is, Lucifer!" "Isn't this what you *used to* always dream about?" "Don't you want to be admired and loved by all women?" "Don't you want your brother to hate and envy you forever?" "You could finally have this for the rest of your life!" "I will make all your dreams come true David." "All you have to do is worship me!" "Do it!" "Do it!" I was cringing because, I was about to sell my soul to Satan. Then the voice of the Holy Spirit said, "Wake up my son!" "Don't you see this is how Satan deceives..." "If you accept Lucifer, you will be a slave to his sin for eternity." "This is how Satan controls society." "He preys on insecurities and fears." "This is all Lucifer has on my children." I woke up and screamed in my mind, "HELL NO SATAN!"

"STOP THE FUCKING CAR!" He got out of my car as a normal person and walked away *rapidly*. This was the hardest decision I have made so far in my life. I remember being drained and exhausted. I am not afraid of the evil one. But I knew this was *just the beginning* of many battles to come!

GOD IS MY BOSS, JESUS IS MY BODYGUARD AND THE HOLY SPIRIT IS MY BEST FRIEND FOREVER...

Do you remember horror movies with vampires that would become werewolves? Werewolves are always compared with evil. Scripture has said, "Beware of the wolf in sheep's clothing."(Matthew 7:15) Within a few weeks after the first temptation, it entered my home. This time, it wanted to scare the life out of me. It was around 3am when I felt a presence in my home. It got cold and my body started shivering as I lay in my bed. Suddenly, a dark shadow appeared to my left. Without looking and with my warrior instinct, I attacked with my *marked* hand. I remember grabbing something. My whole body started convulsing. I looked to my left and saw what looked like a struggling *nasferatu/wolf hybrid* but with the horns and larger teeth!

It was trying to scare the life out of me, but I was not afraid especially after meeting Satan. I asked God to give me a tiny amount of his strength and then gave it one last squeeze. I heard the demonic dog-like yelp. It went away. My whole arm and body was sore and tired for a week.

Six months later, I had my last encounter with a demon. So, I will tell you about the feminine shadow that has haunted me my whole life. It would always wake me up around 3am. I always felt like I was suffocating with something on top of me. I would then go and sleep with my brother because I was scared. I never quite saw what it completely looked like. All I saw was a white shadow and two black eyes. It started happening again when I was fresh out of college. My mom did a cleansing in my apartment so it would go away. God bless my mother. I love her so much. It seemed to work but it came back recently. This time I saw it clearly! You remember the frightening image of the female demon that would come out of the *dead TV* in the movie, "The Ring?" It reminded me of the woman shadow that haunted me my whole life. You see, the devil will use whatever it can to deceive or scare you when you belong to God. It is constantly working against our Lord Almighty. Remember, Lucifer is a fallen angel who wanted to be greater than our Lord

Almighty. It has the greatest GRUDGE against our lord and those who belong. It will use whatever it can to create chaos and fear in the lives of believers! Back to the Ring times a million! It almost worked because I screamed like I never have before. She was standing over my bed on the ceiling. She looked like the *Linda Blair* Exorcist and *the Ring* demon! It was fierce and angry and ready to take my life. I remember thinking as I was yelling, here she finally, is in the flesh!!!

I said, "Jesus please come to my rescue!" This is the demon that has been haunting the *strong men* in my dad's family for generations. She was something that only Jesus could handle. Jesus loves me and is my bodyguard. He did, and she left. I got up from my bed and started walking around my home. I began chanting, "My home is a home of peace and love." "It is a home for God, Jesus and the Holy Spirit." "The spirit of saints like Mother Teresa are all welcome." "This is NO place for darkness and fear." "I am asking my beloved Lord to shun away all evil from my home from this point on and send it back to damnation where it belongs!" "Satan, you and your army are never welcome here!" "You have nothing on me because I am married to my Lord Almighty!" "Don't be jealous of the sanctity of our bond." "Now, never come back into my life till it's time for battle again." "I promise to fight you with NO FEAR!" I am not afraid to die for my lord almighty. As my name is David...I am God's Warrior! After this, my home has been peaceful to this day. Even recently, attempted burglars were caught by police before they left my home. My home had minimal damage. Even the cops were astonished as they questioned me, the victim.

BRING IT SATAN, I AM READY FOR YOU!

It is presently 2018. I have been fine tuning my strength in humility and kindness. I believe Satan has been testing my devotion to God. It will never win. I still go and minister to the homeless with Belinda. Scripture has said, when you give to the poor, you are lending to God. God will indeed repay you with blessings.

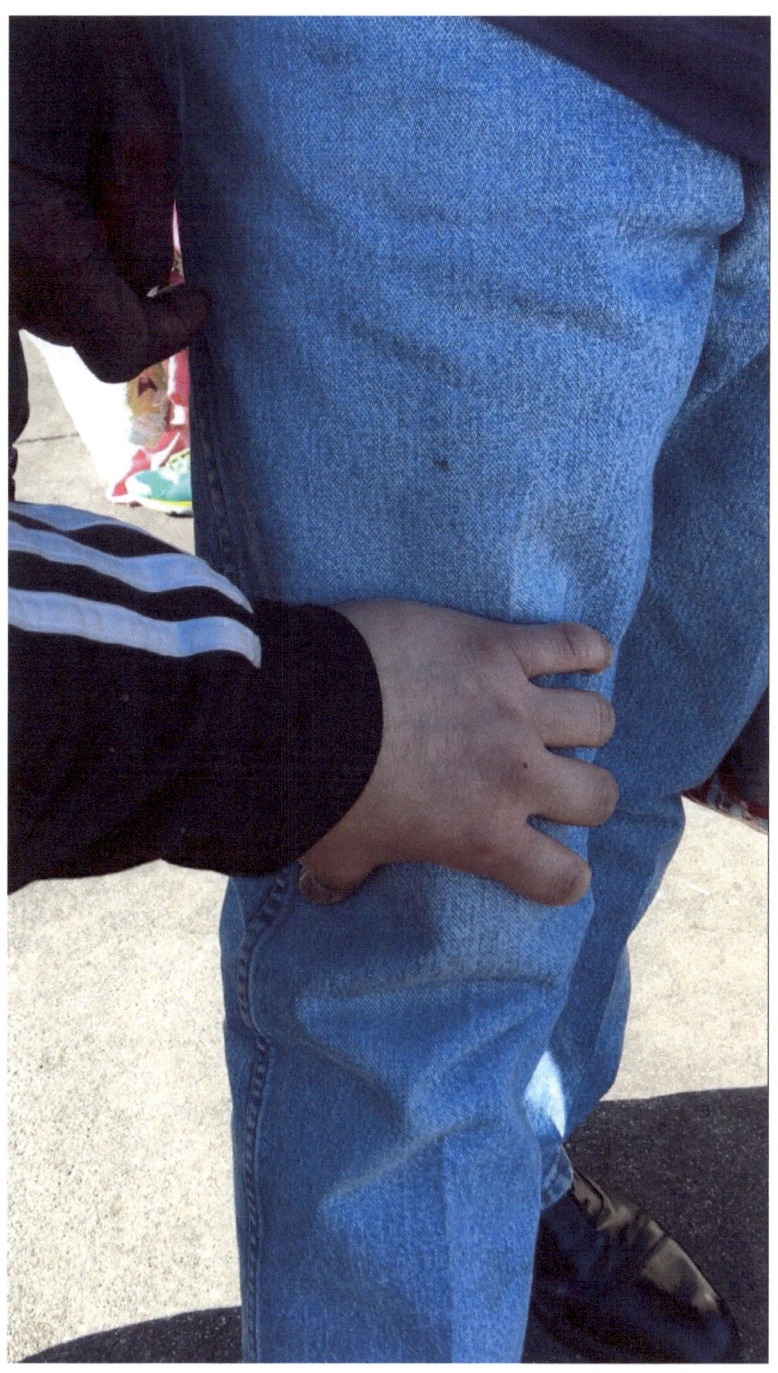

Loving your neighbor as you would yourself is really challenging when it involves a sacrifice. I will only speak of a few miracles that came true because of selfless acts of kindness.

The first act occurred during an uber ride. It was a late Saturday morning and I had 30 minutes before going back to my gym. I got the ride request at the greyhound bus station near my gym. It is easy to practice kindness when it does *not* inconvenience you. So, I hear a knock on my car window and saw an older African American lady and a younger woman with her baby daughter. They had brought some of their suitcases. I got out of my car to help them. They entered my car after putting in the luggage. I then noticed the destination. It said from Austin to Killeen, Texas. I had an appointment at 10 and it was 9:30am. I then looked at the older woman and then she said, "Please don't cancel this ride!" "We have been here since 7am and every rideshare driver has canceled." "Hell no!" "Ditch them!" "Your business is more important." "Kick them out of your car!" "But ...put yourself in their place." "Help them, David..." I called my client to cancel and he was surprisingly gracious. So off we drove to Killeen from Austin. They were very pleasant and full of joy. They were from New Jersey and could only afford to take buses all the way to Austin. It was a long journey. So, the grandma asked me what I had canceled. I told her I was a personal trainer. She was really interested as we discussed her health. Her niece, the younger lady, sat with her child in the back seat. The grandma had several health problems related to her digestion. "Tell her she needs to go back to juicing raw vegetables if she wants to live another 15 years." I asked them if they believed in the Holy Spirit. They said, yes! The Holy Spirit is the counselor God grants you for advice on life. I told her what the Holy Spirit advised me to tell her. She made a face as her niece started laughing. The grandma then told me that she had done it before and it worked. She was miserable though because she loves sweets. They were both astonished that I already knew. The rest of the ride was unbelievable and perfect. There was no traffic and the lights followed us all the way to Killeen. God surrounded us in a bubble of his perfection and joy because we believed in his word. As we approached her daughter's home, the grandma was worried about their aggressive dog. She said that their dog was unruly and very unfriendly and to forgive them for it. I said no worries. We arrived and as soon as the daughter opened her door, the dog flew out barking uncontrollably. The grandma and her niece were screaming at the dog. Instead of attacking me, it jumped into my car and started kissing and playing with me. The dog was smiling at me as it licked my face and I hugged it. I got out of my car as the women watched in awe. I helped the Grandma with the luggage and then gave her one last hug. I also reminded her of God's recommendation. The rest of the ride back to Austin was blessed with thoughts of prophecy of the future. I won't divulge what I saw. God blessed me for being kind. Kindness is a discipline. This world would be a better place if more people would practice kindness.

HUMILITY IS THE GREATEST STRENGTH OF LOVE...

After I became single in December of 2016, I joined Tinder the following January. Most of the middle-aged women on tinder have been through life challenges already. One such woman had 5 children and was a widow. Her husband committed suicide. She was depressed and worried about her youngest son. She asked me if I knew any male mentors for her son. "You don't need this responsibility!" "You have just been through an eight-year relationship and need a break!" "Screw the bitch and her son!" "No, give the widow's son a chance."

"He needs a male figure to give him hope." "Give him hope, my son." I told her to bring him in. His name was J. I felt immediate love for this little 12-year-old boy. "Teach him boxing." I asked him, and he smiled. Within an hour, J was transformed into an amazing boxing machine. It would have taken the average person six months to learn what J picked up within an hour. He easily learned the speed bag, jab and foot work. That was the only time I worked with J. I miss and pray for that boy. I recently spoke to the widow and she told me her son started to believe in himself because of our session. Amazing things will happen with our Lord's blessing! Through God, anything is possible!

WHEN YOU JUDGE, YOU HAVE NO TIME TO LOVE. Thank you, Mother Teresa.

This is the last one I will speak about...Being single has allowed me to work on myself and become closer to God. I try to keep myself busy. I stopped doing rideshare for Uber, but I got involved with Uber Eats. People are always gracious to receive their food. So, I am always in my car during Uber Eats unless I get a request. Sometimes, I need to use the bathroom and it is unbearable. It is not good to hold it in. One rainy night, I had the sudden urge to go to the bathroom. I immediately turned off Uber Eats and drove to a nearby store. I was speed walking into the store when I saw a blind man walking with a cane.

"Fuck him David!" "I hope the stupid man trips and fatally injures his head!" "You need to go to the bathroom!" "No, help him David." "Love your neighbor as you would yourself." "Imagine if I determined you to be blind?" "Go help him." So, I *painfully* walked toward the blind man and asked him if he needed help. The man said, "Yes, I do need help!"   I walked closer to him and asked him to grab my arm. When he did, the awful urge to pee went away!!! We walked into the store and everyone looked at us with instant disgust and judgement. I asked for his name. He told me Benjamin. As we walked to his destination, our great love for Jesus was discussed. He then asked me if I was planning to go to church on Sunday. I said, "Benjamin, I am in church every day because I have God in my heart and spirit." Benjamin smiled and without any knowledge of my name replied, "Good answer, David." I finally led him to his destination and tried not to think too much of what was happening. I was smiling with JOY though because I knew *God was with us and is REAL*!!! I broke down crying with happiness as I walked to my car and drove off.

SO, WHAT DOES ALL THIS MEAN?

Who knows? Why was Jesus persecuted? Back then, *fearful minds could not process the likes of Jesus.* Remember, living in fear is living in the present with Satan. What about the rest of the world? Who is their higher power? *Love will always overcome.* Be impeccable to your word. Never assume. Don't take anything personally and always do your best. Does this ideology create peaceful heavenly thinking? Is this what enlightenment means? Do negative fearful thoughts, darken our auras? Are curanderos enlightened healers? Does enlightened action bring healing to a fearful, dark mindset? After Jesus was baptized by John, he had his epiphany and GOD entered his soul. Jesus was able to see and do things that only God could. He told the truth. Hence, the crucifixion resulted because of *"fear of losing control of the system!"*

WHAT I WOULD DO IF I HAD GOD'S POWER!

With God's power, I would create world peace and fellowship. I would start a *world* movement to end war and pollution. I would encourage the wealthy to contribute. Reward of continued riches would be granted to the participating wealthy. All the sick, starving and poor would have instant mercy, healing and grace from God! I would demand Governments to release the UFO's. The UFO's will collect all nuclear weapons and uranium fuel sources back to their respective planets.

I would ask God to create a harmless insect that eats garbage including plastic. This whole cleansing process would take a year to complete. God would recreate the environment at night. The rain and fertile soils would return just like the beginning. All *wicked mortal sinners* will be commanded to kneel *completely naked* with humility and pray. They will denounce Lucifer and ask for God's forgiveness. The time kneeling will be determined by the degree of wickedness.

Those who don't comply will instantly be taken into hell by Satan's demons.

After the world is cleansed, I will battle Satan as I promised my lord Almighty! It will be a UFC *no rules* battle to the death! It would be viewable by the entire world. Yes, it would be my redemption for my failures as a professional mixed martial artist and to mankind!

THE TRUE MESSAGE.

I am a normal guy who loves God(Jesus). I don't believe in the institution of religion. Love is my religion. It's that simple! The mark on my hand is just a birthmark. The curandero *wanted* to believe something special in her lifetime. God bless her.

Listen...We need to go back to the basics. Be kind. Be humble. Share your passions with one another. It's dangerous to tell a child something, they may or may not be able to process later in life. There are many examples of this mistake. The anointed are the main targets of the evil one.

The four agreements are meant to help us survive socially. Following Jesus and the four agreements would make it hard to *hate*. Worldwide, the *four agreements* should be taught to children from the 5th grade all the way through high school. Understand this! This will change the world. Jesus saved me three years ago. I became *humble enough* to follow this ideology.

Maybe I was crazy and hypersensitive when I met Satan and his demons. That will always be a mystery. It's up to you to buy into this. Nevertheless, *we are all* capable of being like Jesus. We just need to get along and love God with all our heart. *Tales written like movies are* easier to process. If Jesus existed today, would the same outcome have come true? I will always strive to live *God's dream!* This will present many more wonderful challenges and adventures. I challenge you to try it too! Till then, God bless you always.